The GREAT SOUTHWEST

CLB 1245
© 1985 Illustrations and text: Colour Library Books Ltd.,
   Guildford, Surrey, England.
Display and text filmsetting by Acesetters Ltd.,
   Richmond, Surrey, England.
Color separations by Llovet, S.A., Barcelona, Spain.
Produced by AGSA, in Barcelona, Spain.
Printed and bound in Barcelona, Spain by Rieusset and Eurobinder.
All rights reserved.
Published 1985 by Crescent Books, distributed by Crown Publishers, Inc.
Printed in Spain.
ISBN 0 517 460769

The GREAT SOUTHWEST

Text by

MARY DOS-BABA

CRESCENT BOOKS
NEW YORK

As early explorers trudged through the West to chronicle the new land or to search for riches, they often cursed "the horrid mountains" that so stubbornly blocked their path.

Those mountains were truly formidable obstacles. Their steep cliffs and seemingly endless canyons were coursed by a raging river that presented a barrier to many an early pioneer. But, fortunately, not everyone viewed the awesome Grand Canyon in such a dismissive way.

After the Civil War, some scientists and geologists began to think there might be something worthwhile about that marvelous work of nature and, years after explorers had first tried to find routes around the Canyon, Lt. J.C. Ives was ordered to explore the region. His report was considered the first comprehensive study of the Canyon. Ordered by the War Department in 1857, it was commissioned to decide if the Colorado River, which runs through the canyon, was navigable.

After finally reaching the river, tucked deep between the Canyon's walls, Ives was unimpressed. After his trip he wrote, "Ours has been the first and will doubtless be the last party of whites to visit this profitless locality." His geologist on the trip, Dr. John Newberry, did not, however, share the soldier's view of the Canyon. He saw much more in those canyon walls and wrote reports detailing its many features.

It might have been some of his writings which sparked the interest of John Wesley Powell, a geology professor at Illinois Wesleyan University. Although many came before him, it is the explorations of that one-armed, former Union Army Major that are the best-known in Colorado River history.

If it was not for Powell's foresight in realizing that the Grand Canyon was a marvel to behold, it might have been years before Americans understood its wealth as a natural wonder, geologic marvel and one of America's most precious resources.

Today, the Grand Canyon is probably the greatest attraction for visitors to Arizona and the Southwest. But back in 1869, when Powell made his first trip down the untamed Colorado River through the Canyon, his expedition wasn't sure what might be there. After his trip, he did conclude that the Colorado River was not a good commercial channel.

But the beauty and grandeur of the Grand Canyon left its mark on Powell – he realized he could not get enough of it. In fact, his first daring expedition only whetted his appetite and in 1871 he was back trying to solve some more of the mysteries of the Canyon. It was 32 years after his explorations that he wrote, "The glories and the beauties of form, of color and sound unite in the Grand Canyon – form unrivaled even by the mountains, colors that vie with the sunsets, and sounds that span the diapason from tempest to tinkling raindrop, from cataract to bubbling fountain."

It was not long after Powell brought the wonder of the Canyon to public attention that Americans began arriving in the area to see for themselves. Although it was a crude beginning for a tourist business, John Hance scratched a makeshift trail into the Canyon in 1833. He built a cabin and began advertising himself in the Flagstaff paper as a guide.

It did not take others very long to realize there might be something to the Grand Canyon, and a hotel was built at Grandview Point in 1892. Thousands of visitors rode stagecoaches to the area to take a look at nature's handiwork. Travel to the Canyon got easier in 1901, when the Santa Fe Railroad reached the South Rim of the Canyon. The Grand Canyon Village, which sprouted up on the South Rim to meet the needs of visitors arriving by rail, became the center of attraction. Today, the South Rim is still considered the Canyon's gateway, and from that point, millions of visitors each year stand and marvel at the splendor, the open expanses, the gorgeous colors.

When President Benjamin Harrison was a senator from

Indiana, he introduced legislation in 1882, 1883 and 1886 to make the Canyon a National Park. However, his efforts consistently failed because some people feared such a move would hurt economic interests in the area. But, when Harrison was elected president, he took the first step towards preserving the Canyon for posterity. He established, by proclamation, the Grand Canyon Forest Reserve in 1893. That move was followed by the establishment of the Grand Canyon Game Reserve in 1903. Then in 1908 it was declared the Grand Canyon National Monument by President Theodore Roosevelt.

Like so many people who view the Canyon for the first time, when Roosevelt made his first visit in the early 1900s, he was moved by what he saw. He said at the time, "Do nothing to mar its grandeur... keep it for your children, your children's children, and all who come after you, as the one great sight which every American should see." With that thought in mind, other presidents followed in an effort to preserve the area. The Grand Canyon National Park was established by a Congressional Act in 1919 and both Presidents Lyndon B. Johnson and Gerald Ford established new areas as part of the park, enlarging it until it included its present 1,218,375 acres.

Visitors wishing to drink-in the breathtaking beauty of the Grand Canyon today have many more alternatives than the pioneer visitors of the 1800s and early 1900s. A comprehensive view of the Canyon can be had from the air, a real feel for the Canyon's beauty and grandeur can be gained by taking a raft ride down the Colorado River, and an understanding of the Canyon's ruggedness can be obtained with a hike into the Canyon.

And for those who may not have the time or the heart to undertake such explorations, there is always a chance to stop, look and wonder at the harsh and beautiful land that is the Grand Canyon.

At the Visitor's Center on the South Rim are exhibits featuring the geological and historical formation of the Canyon. For those who have the time, it is recommended that they make the effort also to see the Canyon from the North Rim. The North and South Rims are separated by about 11 miles, but the drive from one side to the other is about 215 miles. It is worth the trip, however.

The weather is cooler, the plant life is different and you can peek at the Colorado River below through a hole in the rock known as Angel's Window. Due to snowy conditions, however, the North Rim may be closed from October or November to about April.

On the South Rim, the Grand Canyon Village offers facilities for a brief or a long visit. There are also a number of public campgrounds, lodges and cabins in the area. On the North Rim there are only two facilities: the Grand Canyon Lodge and Cabins and the North Rim Inn.

A plane trip to the Canyon is becoming a popular way to get an understanding of the vast size of the Canyon, which is about 277 river miles long and from four to eighteen miles wide. Several airlines offer such scenic trips, especially from the Phoenix area. For the heartier types there are hiking and mule trips into the Canyon. The mule trips run every day, weather permitting, and the National Park Service says you must be in good physical shape, at least 12 years old and under 200 pounds fully dressed and equipped for the trip. One word of caution: it is not for those who fear heights, because the trip takes riders along some heartstopping trails that look deep into the Canyon. There is a one-day, 12-mile round trip on Bright Angel Trail that takes you to Tonto Plateau. There is also a two-day trip that takes you to Phantom Ranch on the same trail, but returns on the steeper South Kaibab Trail.

For those who plan to venture into the Canyon, it is important to remember that the inner Canyon is a desert. Summer in the Canyon can produce temperatures exceeding 100 degrees and hikers are advised to travel light. Park rangers suggest all hikers gain experience on Bright Angel and Kaibab trails before attempting other trails. Many other trails are old mining routes that have not been maintained. Day hikes into the Canyon are available and reservations are recommended. Each trail is different and, before choosing, hikers should decide what they want to do, such as bird watching or plant hunting, and how long they want to spend on their hike.

"Running the rapids" or taking a trip down the Colorado River through the Canyon, is described by many as the best way to get a real feel for the place. The river trip helps visitors see the Canyon from the bottom and marvel at its many cliffs, canyons, caves, rocks and other features. Rafting down the Colorado also gives the visitor a better understanding of the Canyon's formation, since it is that very river which created it. There are several companies which offer different trip packages, and all of them recommend that reservations be made several months in advance. Whether the Canyon is seen from a lookout point on the South Rim or from a perch high above it in an airplane, visitors are gripped by a sense of wonder of this masterpiece.

"How did it happen?" is the most asked question about this mysterious work of nature. Such a thought was probably running through explorer Powell's mind when he wrote in his *Explorations of the Canyons of the Colorado*, "Thus ever the land is changing; old lands are buried, and new lands are born."

And, thus, the Grand Canyon is ever changing. The Canyon could be considered a geologist's dream, because what happened there over the last several million years is a part of the earth's history.

There have been many detailed studies written on how the Canyon was formed, but most agree that it was produced by erosion – millions and millions of years of it. That erosion, the handiwork of the raging Colorado River, plus the extremes of heat, cold, rains and floods, has made the Canyon what it is today – and what it is becoming. Although it has a rich, exciting history, what is still happening to it every single day provides just as much excitement.

The Colorado River was wild and untamed before modern man conquered it with the construction of dams and lakes. The Spaniards named it the Rio Colorado because it was colored by the sand and mud it swept along with it. From its source high in the Rocky Mountains, down to the Gulf of California, it is 1,450 miles long and with its tributaries drains a land area of more than 240,000 square miles. The roaring Colorado etched its way through the Canyon, changing it and carving it and constantly moving material as it flowed along. The river moved large quantities of sand and boulders and slowly, methodically, wore away layer after layer of rock. It was that erosion and other works of nature that created the cliffs, slopes and caverns that make up the Canyon. At one time the water raced along at up to 12 miles per hour. Now, after construction of the Hoover Dam, the river averages about 4.2 mph, with the rapids ranging between 7.5 and 10 mph.

The Canyon is rich in Indian legends and history and today American Indians live around as well as in the Canyon. The Navajo Indians live on a 16-million-acre reservation which adjoins the eastern boundary of the park. The Havasupai Indians live deep inside it. Havasupai means "people of the blue-green water", and this tribe of about 500 Indians live in an area which is at the bottom of a 3,000-foot drop at the Canyon's west end. The village of Supai, along the clear water of Cataract Creek, is the most inaccessible community in Arizona.

While the Havasupai Tribe has tucked itself away from the fast-moving Arizona lifestyle, many other communities in the state go out of their way to welcome visitors and encourage them to enjoy the many different sights that make up the nation's sixth largest state.

Arizona is a land of contrasts. While it boasts the beauty of the Grand Canyon, it also offers miles and miles of flat desert land. The northern area is dotted with mountains and thick woods of pine, fir and aspen. The southern part of the state has colorful canyons and vast desert areas marked by cactus, rocks and brush. There are ghost towns and large metropolitan cities, old Spanish missions and some of the most luxurious resorts in the West.

Whatever you want, Arizona probably offers it. It is a year-round resort state because, while the southern desert temperatures reach into the 100s in the summer, the northern pines offer a cool, refreshing break from the heat. In winter, the southern desert areas are cool and pleasant, ranging from the 60s to the 80s. The northern areas are cold and provide conditions for skiing and other winter sports. Winter is generally the best time to visit Arizona.

For those who enjoy the hearty outdoors, Arizona is surely their wonderland, with canyons, deserts and mountains to explore. For the more "laid-back" there is a variety of shopping areas, museums and relaxing resorts.

Weather is one of the State's major attractions. It is the nation's sunniest state, receiving 80 percent of the maximum possible sun each year. It boasts an average of 222 clear days.

The area obviously was influenced by the Indians and the Spanish-Mexicans who were its earliest residents. The Indian influence is evident throughout the state, but the change in Arizona has also influenced the Indian settlements, many becoming modern and active communities. Arizona has the largest Indian population of any state, with more than two dozen tribes, most notably the Navajo, Hopi, Pima and Papago.

The Spanish-Mexican influence is also evident in Arizona, particularly in the southern part of the state. One of the most noticeable examples of that influence is in the missions in the area. Father Eusebio Francisco Kino, a Jesuit missionary, founded more than two dozen missions in northern Mexico and southern Arizona.

Water has been and still is another major factor in Arizona's growth. Arizona became a state, the 48th, in 1912, one year before the Theodore Roosevelt Dam was completed near Phoenix. The dam was the first federal reclamation project on the Salt River, and was designed to provide better irrigation for Phoenix. Although that supply of water helped to boost the population in the area around Phoenix, it wasn't until after World War II that Arizona really began to grow. Soldiers who were stationed in the Phoenix area during the war became fascinated with all that the state had to offer. Many returned home only to pack up again and move to

Arizona in hopes of fulfilling their dreams. The influx since that time has led Arizona to become a friendly, informal area where it seems everyone comes from another part of the country, but they are quick to make Arizona their new home and to welcome others.

What has resulted is a growth few ever thought possible. Most of Arizona's growth is concentrated in the "Valley of the Sun" – the heart of Arizona. It includes the state's largest city, Phoenix, and the surrounding communities of Scottsdale, Tempe, Mesa, Chandler, Carefree, Cave Creek, Glendale, Apache Junction and Sun City.

Tucson and its surrounding area, about a two-hour drive south of Phoenix, is also growing by leaps and bounds and offers a more Southwestern flavor.

The Phoenix area has always been considered a winter resort, but more and more people are realizing that the summer is also a good time to enjoy the numerous parks, lakes, lagoons and pools that dot the area. But the nicest thing about the summers in the Valley is that a two to three hour drive will take you north to the cool pines of Payson, Prescott or Sedona.

The Valley of the Sun may surprise some visitors. It is not the barren, brown desert most expect. Rather, there are many green lawns, a wide variety of lush parks and enough golf courses to fulfill any golfer's dreams. The skyline is not made up of skyscrapers but is composed of the various mountains that surround the area: Squaw Peak, Camelback and Mummy Mountains. Valley residents are so proud of this natural skyline that many communities prohibit high-rise buildings in certain areas.

Another attraction for most visitors is the plant life in the Valley. Arizona is the richest state when it comes to cactus. From the tall saguaro cactus – with its arms reaching great heights – to the lowly barrel cactus, Arizona's plant life is fascinating.

While Phoenix is a new city tackling the problems associated with growth, it also is an area that has not forgotten its past. More and more it is trying to restore its historic homes, buildings and schools. Heritage Square, between Sixth and Seventh Streets just south of Monroe in downtown Phoenix, is a restored area where homes such as the Rosson House have taken a step into the past. The houses in the area have been meticulously restored to what they looked like at the turn of the century. The Rosson House was built in 1895 at a cost of $7,525 and has been restored to its full Victorian splendor. Other homes in the area were built in the late 1800s or early 1900s. This quaint area is also the location for many festivities during holiday periods.

Just west of Heritage Square is the Phoenix Civic Plaza, with its lavish Phoenix Symphony Hall and the Convention Center. Further west is the Arizona State Capitol building, with its solid copper dome built in the 1900s. On Capital Mall is the anchor from the USS Arizona, which was sunk in Pearl Harbor during the infamous 1941 attack.

Three museums are a short drive north of the downtown area – the Phoenix Art Museum, the Central Arizona Museum and the Heard Museum. The unique Heard Museum serves as a learning center in Indian cultures. It was founded in 1929 by settlers Maie and Dwight B. Heard, who began collecting American Indian art and artifacts when they arrived in the area in 1895. It has grown from those humble beginnings to being the leading museum in promoting the work of contemporary Native American craftspeople and artists. Although the emphasis of the 75,000 catalogued artifacts is on the culture of Indians of the Southwest, there are many items from other North American tribes. A centerpiece of the museum is U.S. Senator Barry Goldwater's Kachina Doll collection. The museum provides an interesting tour of Indian culture plus a pleasant walk through its buildings and courtyard.

For those who want to know more about Arizona's strange plant life, the Desert Botanical Gardens east of downtown Phoenix in Papago Park is the answer. It offers a leisurely, self-guided tour through the open-air gardens which introduce you to more than 52 desert plants. Founded in 1935 by the Arizona Cactus and Native Flora Society, the gardens are dedicated to educating the public about desert plant life as well as studying and propagating some of the rarer plants. You will see the giant saguaro cactus, varieties of prickly pear cactus, aloe vera plants and the "Old Man of the Desert" cactus, plus much more. But one word of caution – don't touch. It's true, cactus plants are sharp.

Also in Papago Park, not far from the gardens, is the Phoenix Zoo, the largest privately-owned, self-supporting zoo in the United States. Like the Valley of the Sun, the Phoenix Zoo is expanding and adding more exhibits each year. It features the Arabian oryx, one of the world's rarest species, brought to Phoenix Zoo to be saved from extinction. The zoo also has a chilling exhibit of native desert "creepy crawlers," complete with black widow spiders, tarantulas and the Gila monster.

To the west and northwest of Phoenix are the growing communities of Glendale and Peoria, which are more rural and open than Phoenix and their neighbours to the west. Also in that area are the well-known retirement communities of Sun City and Sun City West.

Because Phoenix encompasses such a large area, the best

view can be obtained by looking down on this desert community and its surrounding cities from high atop South Mountain Park. About seven miles south of downtown Phoenix, South Mountain's 16,000 acres of desert constitutes the largest municipal park in the world. It is a great place to become familiar with the desert plant life, since the park has done its best not to intrude on nature. A drive up the winding South Mountain to Dobbins Lookout provides a breathtaking view of the Valley. During the day, the view gives visitors a chance to see the sprawling area, and at night the lookout point provides a spectacular show as the Valley's homes and streets light up.

One of the nice things about the Valley of the Sun is the closeness of the communities. A 20 to 30-minutes drive can take you from Phoenix to Scottsdale, Tempe, Mesa or Chandler – cities with their own distinctive style and charm.

Scottsdale, which calls itself the "West's Most Western Town," is a far cry from a cowboy town. It really is a sophisticated, growing city with some of the finest resorts, restaurants and shopping areas in the Valley. One of the best ways to reach Scottsdale from Phoenix is to drive across Lincoln Drive and pass through the town of Paradise Valley. The small town of PV is probably one of the more luxurious in the country. Exclusive, sprawling homes have been built on the sides of Camelback and Mummy Mountains and a drive through the area gives visitors a taste of the "good life" in the Valley. It is also the home of one of Arizona's most famous residents, U.S. Senator Barry Goldwater, as well as several other celebrities, sports figures and musicians.

Of course, once you hit the city of Scottsdale it is often hard to tell you have left Paradise Valley because Scottsdale is also known for its beautiful homes, especially in the growing north area. Downtown Scottsdale, in the southern end of the city, is a shopper's delight. With the variety of stores in Fifth Avenue and the Old Scottsdale areas, some shoppers need go no further to find the buy of their dreams. The stores in Fifth Avenue, which number in the hundreds, offer a range of the finest in art galleries, jewelry and clothing stores and antique shops. But there are also T-shirt and trinket stores to meet all your buying needs. The area is much more than one avenue, and it provides a lovely walk through part of the city.

On the other side of Scottsdale Road is the Old Scottsdale shopping area, with a more Western flavor to its shops. A walk through this area also gives you a peek into Scottsdale's rich past. There is an 1880s blacksmith shop, a mission church and the Little Red Schoolhouse, which is now home to the Scottsdale Chamber of Commerce. This mingling of the old and new makes for an enjoyable way to get a feel for Scottsdale. Not far from Old Scottsdale is the city's Civic

Center Plaza, with the Scottsdale Center for the Arts, City Hall and the Scottsdale Mall. It is complete with fountains and gardens and is the city's shining example of its dedication to providing the best.

The city prides itself on its reputation as an arts and cultural center, and proof of that is seen throughout the Civic Center area with its many sculptures, and in the numerous art galleries in the city as well as in the Cosanti Foundation. The foundation is a non-profit-making, educational organization founded by Paolo Soleri and is based in Scottsdale. Soleri is best known for his work at Arcosanti, which is an energy-efficient town built by the Cosanti Foundation near Cordes Junction, north of Phoenix. Arcosanti is a prototype of Soleri's communal concept he calls Arcology, a term he used to describe the concept of architecture and ecology working as an integral process. Each year, students and professionals come to work on the site and attend seminars. Visitors can also tour both Cosanti and Arcosanti and watch the work being done there, including the handcrafting of Soleri bells and sculptures.

Scottsdale is a long, narrow city and most of the growth and change in the city is taking place in its northern area. It was once considered "the middle of nowhere," dotted with large horse ranches and open desert. But today a drive "up north" will prove how the city is growing. Most of the ranches are now large developments of lovely homes, and shopping areas and restaurants have sprung up to meet the needs of the new population. One holdover to the more rustic days in the city is at Rawhide, in north Scottsdale. It is a re-created Western town complete with shoot-outs in the streets, hay rides and wooden sidewalks.

Also in this area is Taliesin West, which was built by Frank Lloyd Wright and is now the winter home of his architectural foundation. Taliesin carries out Wright's theme of harmonizing design with nature. Tours of Taliesin are available. Nearby are the communities of Carefree, Cave Creek and Fountain Hills.

Probably the best way to understand the unique city of Scottsdale is to look at how it has handled its problem of flooding. Because the ground is unusually hard and dry, even a minor rainstorm can send water rushing through the natural washes. Scottsdale had just such a problem with a wash – Indian Bend Wash – which runs almost through the center of the city. Most of these types of problems are handled with a concrete-lined channel to direct the flood water to the river. But Scottsdale officials and residents could not stand the idea of such a channel marring the city. After years of work, what has resulted is the Scottsdale Indian Bend Wash Greenbelt. The city and the U.S. Army Corps of

Engineers worked to make the wash a greenbelt of parks, bike paths and lakes, all designed to serve two purposes – flood control and recreation. Where most cities would have opted for the simple flood-control plan, Scottsdale was committed to making a flooding problem a benefit to the city.

South of Scottsdale is another growing city, one which is trying to emphasize its roots. Tempe, home of Arizona State University, is a residential community with a downtown area that is being revived. Tempe is dotted by many shopping centers, but it is focusing its redevelopment efforts on its historical downtown area. Mill Avenue is being restored to its turn-of-the-century look and many stores and restaurants in the area are doing their part in bringing back the city's history. But Mill Avenue is an exciting shopping district and quite a night spot, especially when the university is in session.

The cultural opportunities in Tempe are great, due in large part to the university and its Grady Gammage Center, the last architectural masterpiece of Frank Lloyd Wright. And for the sports fan, Tempe is the focal point for college football, baseball and basketball action. Each year, Tempe is host to the Fiesta Bowl game.

The city of Mesa, east of Tempe, was founded by Mormon pioneers about 100 years ago, and the Mormon tradition is still strong in this city. The Mormon pioneers were responsible for the noticeably wide streets in the city – they wanted to be sure a team of four horses could turn around in the streets.

One of the main attractions in Mesa is the Mormon Temple, which is closed to the public but free guided tours describe the attractive buildings and the gardens. The Mesa Museum is an interesting stop, especially for the children. It offers a hands-on history and archeology exhibit, emphasizing the Southwest. It also has the largest collection of branding irons in the world.

East of Mesa is the Apache Trail, which, because of its closeness to the metropolitan area, should not be passed up. It is one of the most scenic drives in the Valley and affords breathtaking view of the desert. The trail is a portion of Highway 88 that twists and turns through the Superstition Mountains from Apache Junction to Roosevelt Lake and then on to Globe. The first 18 miles are paved, taking visitors by Canyon Lake and the tiny community of Tortilla Flat. The final leg of the trail to Roosevelt Dam is unpaved but is passable for most vehicles.

The Apache Trail had its humble beginning as just that – a trail. It was etched out of the rough desert mountain to bring supplies to the construction site at Roosevelt Dam in the early 1900s. The dam is the largest masonry dam in the world. Looking at the structure it is hard to imagine how workers got their supplies to the site over the windy, dusty, narrow Apache Trail.

Theodore Roosevelt was driven up the trail in an open touring car to make the dedication speech at the dam. Despite the difficult conditions, Roosevelt was able to see the majesty of the area. "It is the most awe-inspiring and most sublimely beautiful panorama nature has ever created," Roosevelt said. Anyone who travels that trail today will have an easier trip than Roosevelt, but they also will see the quiet, majestic, breathtaking landscape.

On the way to the trail, just about five miles from the town of Apache Junction, is the Lost Dutchman State Park on the slopes of the Superstition Mountains. The park is a 300-acre desert park named after German prospector Jacob Walz, who carries the legendary nickname "The Dutchman."

The Superstitions are a beautiful, alluring mountain range. Maybe it is the name or the tales about them, but they look mysterious. And when the sun hits them a certain way, they are almost eerie. The Apache Indians, the first inhabitants of the area, claimed the Superstitions were the land of evil spirits. Although the stories surrounding the Dutchman and the mountains are just that – tales – people today still go hunting for "gold in them thar hills." The allure of the beautiful mountains is based on the legend of that crusty old prospector who claimed to have found gold there. Legend has it that he would leave his great gold find every now and then to have a few drinks in the desert town of Phoenix. He told of his gold treasures to anyone who listened and many of his drinking companions tried to follow him back into those mountains. Many of them were lucky if they came out empty-handed, for most never made it out of the mountains alive. Walz had the misfortune of dying before he could tell anyone exactly where the gold was. He reportedly sketched a map to his find, however. Well, that map keeps showing up and many a gold-eyed prospector has followed its trail. Walz's great gold find has never been rediscovered despite all the maps which claim to the "the real one." But if you can put visions of gold aside, you will see the Superstitions for what they are – a beautiful mountain range to view and explore.

No matter where you stay or visit in the Valley of the Sun, there is a variety of resorts, hotels, motels and restaurants to meet every need and every pocketbook. Besides the luxurious Biltmore Hotel, Camelback Inn and Pointe Resorts there are more moderately priced places to stay. And when it comes to dining out you can have elegance or fast-food, for there are literally hudreds of restaurants in the Valley.

Many people associate Arizona with cowboys and the Wild West. A look at the state in the 1980s will reveal a tamed West with just a few cowboys roaming what range is left. But a look into the wild days of the past can be found in and around Tucson. For the Wild West enthusiast there is Old Tucson and Tombstone.

Tombstone is the "town too tough to die," but during its rough and tumble days many a tough man died in its streets. It was the wildest town in the West back then; a town which grew up thanks to silver mines in the area. Tombstone is probably best known for its OK Corral, where the infamous Earp brothers and Doc Holliday shot it out with the Clantons in the most famous gun battle of all time.

Tombstone has a tough past and that has been preserved. Visitors can walk through the town today and view its many landmarks, and if they really use their imaginations they can probably hear gunshots ringing out in the streets. To get a feel for Tombstone visitors should visit Boot Hill graveyard, where many a notorious bad man is buried; the OK Corral; the Bird Cage Theater; the old County Courthouse, now a museum; and the office of the old *Tombstone Epitaph* newspaper, which detailed the good and bad times of Tombstone.

If Tombstone doesn't quench your thirst for the Old West, there is Old Tucson, created in 1939 for the movie "Arizona." Since that time it has been the setting for about 100 films, TV shows and commercials. This re-created 1860s Western town is now a major attraction for visitors who want a taste of the days when gunfighters roamed the dusty streets and the stagecoach was a luxurious form of transportation. It is a real treat for children as well as the child in all of us.

Old Tucson is about 12 miles from the heart of present-day Tucson and has an authentic stageline ride (but be careful of masked gunmen), a ride through the Iron Door Mine and many other attractions.

Before people began fighting it out on the streets of Tombstone and other boom towns in and around Tucson, a Jesuit missionary roamed the area, exploring and mapping the Southwest region and establishing missions. Padre Eusebio Francisco Kino founded more than two dozen missions in northern Mexico and southern Arizona. The surviving monuments to his work are the Mission San Xavier del Bac, about nine miles south of Tucson, and Tumanacori, part of the national monument north of Nogales.

Padre Kino first came to the Tucson area in 1691. In 1700 he laid the foundation for his first church, which stood about two miles north of the existing mission. The mission which survives today was constructed during a 14-year period from 1783 to 1797. The brilliant white dome and lofty towers of the mission stand out elegantly in the desert. The only wood used in the adobe building is in the window and door frames. Every corner of this "White Dove of the Desert" is beautifully painted. The work and loving care that went into the construction of this mission more than 200 years ago is evident in its every detail. There is also a mystery about the museum since little is known about the architecture, its builders or the reason why one of the towers was never completed. Some say the tower was left unfinished in order to avoid a Spanish tax on finished churches. It is these details that are left to the mind of the modern visitor who comes to enjoy this early monument in the desert.

One of the most famous artists associated with Arizona is the late Ted DeGrazia. He is known for his colorful paintings of shy-looking Indian children and his work has become famous worldwide. DeGrazia's Gallery in the Sun, operated by the DeGrazia Art and Cultural Foundation, was designed by him and constructed not only under his supervision but in some cases with his own hands. The gallery is on north Swan Road, north of Downtown Tucson.

The gallery is made up of adobe buildings with rooms exhibiting some DeGrazia originals. Derazia also included in the gallery a lovely chapel built in honor of Padre Kino. It was the first building completed on the location and all the material used in it, including the water needed for construction, were hauled to the site by DeGrazia in his car. He painted murals on the interior walls which truly are priceless works.

The visitor who has become a cactus lover after seeing the unique plants throughout the area should not miss the Arizona Sonara Desert Museum, west of Tucson, and the Saguaro National Monument, which lies both east and west of the city.

The museum is near Old Tucson and allows people to see desert plant life and animals in their natural settings. It is a combination botanical garden and zoo, unmatched in its efforts to give visitors a peek into nature. You can watch otters and beavers romping in their natural surroundings, walk in an aviary and hold docile desert tortoises. One thing you learn from the desert museum and the nearby Saguaro National Monument is that the desert is not a barren wasteland, but a unique growth area rich in animal and plant life. The national monument includes 123 square miles, made up of its western section near the desert museum and the older, original portion of the monument, 16 miles east of Tucson. The older section has a Visitor's Center with exhibits about the area and a loop drive through the monument.

Calling this area a monument may be a little confusing: it is basically a saguaro forest. The number of saguaros and other cacti in this forest can't be counted – they stand like an army of tall soldiers literally covering the sloping hills.

The saguaro has a large, thick, fluted trunk with arms jutting up to great heights. It can reach up to 50 feet and weigh 12 tons. It is often hard to determine the age of a saguaro, but many live to be 100 or 200 years old. The saguaro, being a desert plant, has a natural water storage system, hoarding the small, precious amounts of desert rainfall. When it rains, the saguaro drinks up the moisture and stores it in its pulpy tissue. A mature cactus can store as much as eight tons of moisture after the rainy season. As the saguaro's water supply expands, so does its trunk. As it uses that water during the long, dry months, the trunk contracts and the saguaro becomes thinner. And not only is the saguaro a practical plant, it is also beautiful, with a creamy white blossom sprouting on its top in May or early June. This night-flowering blossom is Arizona's state flower.

While the Tucson area offers beautiful desert scenery, it doesn't stop there. Mount Lemmon, in the Santa Catalina Mountains, is a great summer gateway and in the winter it is the southernmost ski area in the United States. A drive up to Mount Lemmon takes you through an area of cactus and desert landscape, then through tall, lean Ponderosa pine and finally to Douglas fir and aspen. There is great scenery all around, picnic areas, fishing spots and at the top is the Mount Lemmon ski area, where you can ride the ski lift any time of year for a breathtaking view of the area.

For those who enjoy looking at the scenery around them but can't help looking up at the skies and wondering about the starry scenery above, Kitt Peak National Observatory is for them. It is 50 miles southeast of Tucson and is a complex of research facilities operated in cooperation with 17 universities. Tours are offered to the public and at the observatory you will see some of the largest telescopes in the world.

Tucson is also a good "home base" for seeing other areas in the southern part of the state, such as the old copper mines of Bisbee, and for traveling into Mexico.

The area of Arizona between the Valley of the Sun and the Grand Canyon presents a different picture of this state of contrasts.

An easy drive north of Phoenix takes you to such summer escape spots as Payson, Sedona, Oak Creek, Prescott and the Verde Valley. The closest to Phoenix is Payson, a small town with shops and resorts. It is a charming area for exploring the surrounding pine country. Just outside Payson is the Tonto Natural Bridge, the largest natural bridge in the world. It stands 183 feet above Pine Creek and is about 400 feet long, providing living proof that Mother Nature is still the best engineer.

Novelist Zane Grey often spoke of the Tonto Rim in his adventure stories. What he was referring to is the Mogollon (pronounced muggy-yone) Rim outside Payson. The rim, as it is called, is a mixture of rock and timber, stretching nearly 300 miles into New Mexico. It separates the plateau country from the low country. Those who enjoy the outdoors can spend hour after hour exploring the many different features in and around the Payson area and the rim.

Without doubt, some of the loveliest scenery in Arizona outside of the Grand Canyon is in Oak Creek Canyon and Sedona. It is known as Red Rock country and one look at the area will explain why. Oak Creek and Sedona are hedged by brilliant red sandstone "walls" that reach high into the air, creating a vivid contrast with the clear blue sky. It is landscape that is hard to match for the drama it provides in both color and design. If you want to explore the area leisurely and take in its beauty there are many places for hiking and picture-taking. If you feel like staying in the Red Rocks for a while, there are several motels, hotels and cabins available. Because Sedona is a year-round resort, it has many shopping areas and restaurants. One of the more popular attractions is Tlaquepaque, a colonial Mexican village with a collection of craft shops, galleries and restaurants. Nestled high in the red rocks of Sedona is the Chapel of the Holy Cross, which is an integral part of a 250-foot, twin-pinnacled spur that protrudes from a rock wall. The chapel was first sketched in 1932 by Marguerite Straube and it was to be built in Budapest. However, the war put an end to that project and it finally found its unique home in the majestic rocks of Sedona.

Further to the north is Flagstaff. The largest city in the north country, it is the home of Northern Arizona University and is a stopping place for many on their way to visit the Grad Canyon or to enjoy the northern ski areas. It offers a small-town atmosphere but has many nice hotels and restaurants.

One of the most historic towns in Arizona's north country is Prescott, which was the capital of the Arizona Territory at two different times. In the middle of town is an old stone courthouse, and across the street from that is famous Whiskey Row, where a great many saloons lined the street in those "good ole Territorial days." History is an important part of Prescott's attraction and this is evident in the Arizona Pioneers Home, a home for the men and women who remember the state when it was a territory. Another point of interest in Prescott is the Sharlot Hall Museum, which was the governor's mansion, built of logs in 1864.

Another part of Arizona's varied past can be found in the charming town of Jerome, noth of Prescott in the Verde Valley. It is a great example of a copper boom town that went bust. At one time, this town was among Arizona's largest cities, producing $800 million worth of copper in 72 years. Today, Jerome is an attraction for people who want to see a living ghost town. Tough Jerome residents were not about to let this little town on the side of a mountain just waste away. It is now a delightful collection of shops and restaurants and restored homes. There is a Mine Museum which gives visitors an idea of how dangerous mining was in its early days.

By definition, the word desert means an arid region lacking in water. While a great deal of Arizona is desert, the state has made good use of the rivers that flow through it with the construction of dams and lakes. At times, it is hard to believe that water is a scarce commodity in Arizona.

The Salt River in the Phoenix area has four dams and the Verde River has two. These dams serve the very practical purposes of supplying hydro-electric power and providing water storage. But the lakes that have been formed behind them give Arizona recreational areas for boating, swimming and fishing. The land surrounding the lakes is used for picnicking and enjoying the outdoors. The popular lakes are Apache Lake, Canyon Lake and Saguaro Lake, all of which are along the Apache Trail. They are a nearby cooling spot for Valley of Sun residents during the summer. In the northern areas of the state there are more dams and recreational lakes, including one which has the London Bridge across it. Lake Havasu is the result of water backing up behind Parker Dam. North of the city of Yuma, in the southwestern part of the state, Lake Havasu City was built on the shores of the lake. Unlike most Arizona cities and towns with their roots deep in history, Lake Havasu City is a new city which was actually created by Robert P. McCulloch.

McCulloch decided in the 1960s to move his chain saw factory out of Los Angeles to a better climate. He picked the Lake Havasu area which was growing as Arizona and California fought to attract visitors to their side of the lake. McCulloch was also responsible for bringing the London Bridge to Lake Havasu City, which is now a major attraction. He bought the landmark for $2.46 million and then spent another $5 to $6 million to bring it, stone by stone, to Arizona. Thanks to McCulloch and his bridge, the area has flourished. A European-style international village has sprung up around the bridge, with quaint shops and restaurants, and its proximity to the lake has made it a mecca for boaters and fishermen.

Still further north is the Hoover Dam and the popular recreation area created by its lakes, Meade and Mohave,

which Arizona shares with Nevada. At the northernmost edge of the state is Lake Powell, the centerpiece of the Glen Canyon National Recreation Area. The lake was created by the Glen Canyon Dam, which was constructed in the 1950s, the newest of the dams on the Colorado River. Lake Powell is surrounded by high canyon walls and a jagged shoreline. Tours of the area are offered, and Lake Powell is a popular lake for houseboats and powerboats, both of which can be rented for full days, half days or longer. But, because of its popularity, reservations are recommended. An interesting sidetrip in the area is to the Rainbow Bridge, the world's largest natural rock span. It is so tall, the dome of the U.S. Capitol could fit underneath it.

While Tucson has its monument preserving the statuesque saguaro cactus, further to the southwest is the Organ Pipe national Monument. It is covered by the unusual-looking organ pipe cactus as well as palo verde trees and other desert plants. The organ pipe cactus, so named because its arms look like pipes of a church organ, stands out in this desert garden. There is a visitor's center at the monument which provides information on driving and hiking through this preserved area.

Some of the most interesting monuments in Arizona give visitors a look into ancient Indian dwellings. The ones closest to Phoenix are the Casa Grande Ruins National Monument to the south of Phoenix and Montezuma Castle to the north. The Casa Grande ruin, a four-story tower with solid mud walls, served as both a dwelling and lookout for the village. It is believed the ruin reflects the influence of both the Hohokam and the Pueblo Indians. The ruin, more than 900 years old, is now protected by a great roof built by the National Park Service because the ancient structure was eroding. Montezuma Castle is not really a castle but an "ancient tenement house." It is built on a naturally eroded hollow on the cliff of Beaver Creek. The ruins are in almost perfect condition and, with a little imagination, visitors can almost see the people who occupied its 20 rooms in the five-story complex. The ancient dwellers apparently farmed by day, and at night climbed ladders to the security of their cliff homes. The monument is easily accessible and has a visitor's center. About seven miles from the monument is the Montezuma Well, where you can see the tribe's irrigation system.

In the Verde Valley, near Clarkdale, is the Tuzigoot National Monument, which includes the ruins of an ancient "town" considered home to dwellers from 1100 to 1450 A.D. A museum at the monument displays the pottery and other artifacts discovered when the ruins were excavated in the 1930s. Tuzigoot has about 110 large rooms and entrance was gained by climbing ladders. As with most of these ancient dwellings, little is known about the people who lived in them or what drove them from the security of their homes.

If you enjoy gathering items of trivia, you will like the Four Corners National Monument. It is the only place in the United States where four states touch – Arizona, New Mexico, Colorado and Utah. After visiting the Four Corners monument, which has the names and seals of the four states, you can tell your friends you stood in two states at the same moment.

The largest Indian reservation in Arizona, the Navajo reservation, is near the Four Corners area and is worth a stop for anyone who wants to get a feel for today's American Indians. Visitors must remember that once they enter the reservation they are on Indian land, which is governed by an Indian Tribal Council, an Indian police force and Indian courts and judges. Visitors should honor the dignity of the tribe on its reservation and should respect their customs. The Navajo Indians display a mix of old tribal customs and new, modern ways. The deeper you go into the large reservation, the more you will see the Indian in his or her native dress, performing the age-old crafts of weaving and jewelry-making.

No one should leave Arizona without seeing its Painted Desert and the Petrified Forest National Park. The Painted Desert, which is not far from the Navajo community, is an amazing sight. Millions of years ago, the desert was the floor of an ocean and was stained or dyed by its mineral-rich water. After nature changed the ocean into a desert, it left behind cliffs and miles and miles of sand tinted with every color of the rainbow. And if that is not enough to attract attention, the Painted Desert also contains "the forest that was" – the Petrified Forest National Park, at the southern end of the Painted Desert. The park, first preserved as a monument under the Antiquities Act, contains some of the brightest and most colorful concentrations of petrified wood ever found. In fact, the petrified wood found in the forest is so colorful that one area is nicknamed the Rainbow Forest.

The stone trees which grace this forest have a past that dates back millions of years. Although the forest has a mysterious nature, the happenings that created it can be mapped. When the trees were alive, they were uprooted and swept down river, and buried in the sand and mud in the spots where they now rest. During their trip, the trees lost their bark, branches and roots. Then something happened that caused the wood to become petrified rather than to decay. A distant volcano spewed clouds of fine cinders which were carried by the wind and deposited on the mud and sand where the wood is buried. This occurred over and over, providing the silica needed to petrify the wood. All of this also helped to create the rainbow

of colors that stretch through the area. The wood contains quartz crystal, clear amethyst and pieces of amber.

If Arizona has whetted your appetite for the flavor of the Southwest, then nearby Nevada and New Mexico offer a more complete look at this growing area of the country.

Nevada calls itself the Entertainment Capital of the World and, thanks to the city of Las Vegas, that is probably true. Most visitors, however, think Nevada is nothing more than the glittering gambling city of Vegas, but it is much more. The cities of Virginia City and Carson City are rich in history. Reno and Lake Tahoe offer some of the most beautiful scenery and the spectacular Hoover Dam and its Lakes Mead and Mohave are great recreation areas.

But there is no doubt that Las Vegas, with its neon lights and plush resorts, is Nevada's ace in the hole. Las Vegas had a quiet beginning which gave no hint at what it would become. It was established in 1855 as a Mormon settlement. The Mormons tried their missionary work among the Indians of the area, but they soon abandoned their efforts. For several years, Las Vegas remained a sleepy town, but the arrival of the railroad in 1905 gave a boost to the area. During the Depression, it got another boost with the construction of Hoover Dam and, of course, the legalization of gambling.

The Strip in Vegas is known throughout the world. It is where some of the better-known hotels and casinos are concentrated in a 3½ mile block. Las Vegas never sleeps. It keeps the doors to its casinos open 24 hours a day, every day, and more than 15 million people each year visit this glitter palace. Besides the gambling, Vegas is known for its entertainment – from the high kicking showgirls to world-famous singers and comedians.

Although Las Vegas is a city of neon, it is also a city with homes, schools, churches and a university. It is the most populated area of the state and also offers visitors a number of theme and amusement parks, historical exhibits at the Old Mormon Fort and at the Nevada State Museum and Historical Society. Outside of this entertainment capital is a variety of attractions including Red Rock Canyon and Hoover Dam. Red Rock Canyon is a 3,000-foot escarpment created by a geologic fault. You can take a scenic drive through the area to look at the lovely desert sights and wildlife.

Hoover Dam may not sound like an exciting place, but it is a wonder that has to be seen to be believed and appreciated. Considering this flood-control project was built in 1935 and took five years to complete, the dam was quite an undertaking in its time. It holds 3½ million cubic yards of concrete and is 660 feet thick at its base and 45 feet thick at the crest. It is 726 feet from bedrock to the top roadway. It took 1,200 men to build the dam, then the biggest in the world.

While taming the once-raging Colorado River, Hoover Dam created the Lake Mead National Recreation Area with the water stored behind it. Both Lake Mead and Lake Mohave are part of the recreation area, which is on the Arizona-Nevada border. The area offers boating, swimming, fishing, water skiing, hiking and camping. The lakes also provide a beautiful scenic area, since they are bordered by rocks, hills and sandy beaches.

Nevada is one of the fastest growing states, but also one of the most sparsely populated. Besides the Las Vegas area, the only other highly concentrated population center is in the Reno area at the wester edge of the state. In the area around Reno is Lake Tahoe, Virginia City and Carson City.

While the focal point of the state today is Las Vegas and Reno, in the 1800s, Virginia City was Nevada's hot spot for more than 20 years. It was built over the richest mine in the Comstock Lode, which was named after prospector Henry Comstock. Wealth from the rich silver lode is famous for helping to finance the Union army during the Civil War and to re-build San Francisco after its devastating earthquake.

In 1863, Virginia City was the second largest city in the West. It was a bustling, rowdy town with more than 100 saloons, dozens of stores, banks, six churches and a busy railroad system. Most of the historic buildings standing today date from 1879 because in 1875 a fire destroyed half the town. But Virginia City was tough – and rich – so it quickly got on its feet again. However, in typical boomtown fashion, by the end of the 1870s Virginia City was on the decline because the money from the famous silver lode had stopped flowing. What were once boarding homes and saloons in the town are now museums, shops and restaurants. Thanks to the preservation of some of the historic Victorian homes and other buildings, visitors can understand what Virginia City was like in its heyday.

When Virginia City exploded into growth after the discovery of silver, Reno developed into a supply town for the area. Reno is on the edge of the Truckee Meadows, but it no longer exists just to serve Virginia City. It was legalized gambling and the liberalization of divorce laws which pushed Reno into the limelight. Tourism is its livelihood today and it has some of Nevada's finest casinos. Reno is not simply casinos, however, it also has numerous golf courses, as well as the Nevada Historical Society Museum, the famous gun collection at Harold's Club and Harrah's Automobile City in nearby Sparks.

Carson City, named after frontier scout Kit Carson, is also tied to Virginia City and its silver lode. Carson City, 16 miles northeast of Virginia City, is Nevada's state capital. In addition to the brown sandstone capitol building with its silver dome, visitors can take a walk through Nevada's rich past at the Nevada State Museum, the Virginia-Truckee Railroad Museum, and many restored Victorian homes.

While Reno has the casinos and nightlife, and Virginia and Carson cities have the history, the nearby Lake Tahoe area is rich in scenery and outdoor fun. One third of the lake is in Nevada and the rest is in California. It is an alpine lake, one of the deepest in the world. Lake Tahoe is 22 miles long, 12 miles wide and has a shoreline of 72 miles. Its fresh, clear blue water makes it a spectacular sight as well as a great recreation area.

For those who enjoy the wide open spaces, Nevada will surely please. Fishing is good in the state with its more than 300 miles of lakes, rivers and streams; water sports are popular in the Lake Mead area; and winter brings hundreds to Nevada for skiing in the Sierra Nevada range around Lake Tahoe. There are many old mining camps, monuments and ghost towns in the state. A drive around Nevada will turn up such diverse finds as Ichthyosau State Park, with the remains of a giant sea reptile; Diana's Punch Bowl, a 30-foot-wide geyser, and Lehman Caves, a series of cool and colorful underground caves.

New Mexico offers the best blend of the new and old in the Southwest. On one hand it has Indian ruins dating back to 600 A.D. and the charming city of Santa Fe, which has its roots in the 1600s. On the other hand, New Mexico is firmly planted in the 20th century thanks to the growth of Albuquerque, its largest city, and its participation in the field of nuclear and space research.

New Mexico has a rich Spanish and Indian tradition and has maintained this heritage despite the fact that the state is growing and changing rapidly. Tourism is now New Mexico's third most important industry. While the state has a strong sense of tradition, some people consider the birth of New Mexico to date from July 16, 1945, when the world's first atomic bomb was detonated near Alamogordo. The crater made by the explosion is in a part of southern New Mexico named by the Spanish years ago – Jornado del Muerto – Journey of the Dead.

Albuquerque is an enchanting city, with its Old Town area, and the towering Sandia Mountains providing a backdrop. It is a good base city for traveling to other points of interest in the state. But first visitors should drink in the beauty in and around Albuquerque. When arriving in the city you can't help but notice the Sandia Mountains about 24 miles northeast. Sandia Peak juts 10,000 feet into the air, towering over this expanding city. These mountains are the home of mythical Indian deities and they look over the heart of the state. The mountains provide a cool summer retreat and are a mecca for winter sports enthusiasts. The great thing about Sandia peak is you can get a close up look at this scenic mountain. The Sandia Peak tram is the world's longest continuous tramway. Completed in 1966, the tram takes visitors on a 2.7 mile ride up to Sandia Peak. The scenery on the way is wonderful and at the top it gets even better. At the top of the peak is the Sandia Ski Area as well as the plush High Finance Restaurant, where you can dine and enjoy the scenery.

Albuquerque is also the home of the University of New Mexico, the Albuquerque Museum of Art, History and Science, and its quaint Old Town area on the western edge of the city.

A visit to Old Town gives visitors a feel for what Albuquerque was and what it is becoming. It is a city rich in history, founded in 1706, but striving to be a popular city offering many attractions to visitors. Walking through the narrow streets of Old Town and into its Spanish-style plaza provides a look at the Albuquerque of the past. But the unique gift shops and restaurants that line the streets remind visitors that the city is there for their pleasure.

North of Albuquerque is New Mexico's richest historical city, Santa Fe. Its roots reach back into the 1600s, when it was founded as the Capital of New Spain. It is a charming community with its adobe structured State Capitol building sitting at the foot of the Sangre de Cristo Mountains. The best way to tour this rich cultural city is to walk in the area around the plaza and view such historical buildings as the Palace of Governors, an adobe building more than 350 years old, the Museum of Fine Arts, and Our Lady of Light Chapel with its "miraculous" staircase, which has no nails or visible means of support.

Further north of Santa Fe is the Village of Taos, long considered an "art colony", where hundreds of artists and craftspeople live and work. There are many galleries and shops along the town's winding streets. Taos also offers some of the finest winter skiing in the state.

New Mexico is more than just its cities and towns; outside its population area there are many Indian ruins, recreation areas and ghost towns.

In northwest New Mexico are the ruins of two Indian pueblos, the Aztec Ruins National Monument and Chaco Canyon. The Aztec ruin is one of the largest of the old pueblo towns, dating back to 1100 A.D. The largest ruin at Chaco Canyon, Pueblo Bonito, is considered one of the most beautiful ruins in the Southwest. Built in the shape of the letter D, the ruin is four to five stories high, with walls made of smooth sandstone. It had 800 rooms and about 1,200 inhabitants when pre-Columbian Indians lived there around 600 A.D.

Two interesting and unusual sights in the state are the White Sands National Monument near Alamogordo and the Carlsbad Cavern National park. The White Sands Monument looks like nothing more than large sand dunes at first glance. But the sand dunes are actually piles of powdered alabaster which constantly shift with the southwestern winds.

Carlsbad Caverns are considered the greatest of all caves. They include seven miles of corridors and chambers which are open to the public. How the caves were constructed by nature is a complicated story of geology, but anyone can appreciate what happened in the caves when they see the breathtaking sculptures of stone and the delicate colors throughout.

Whether you are interested in caves or canyons, metropolitan cities or ancient Indian dwellings, glittering casinos or nature's quiet beauty, the Southwest has it. The area is a land of contrasts which offers visitors a peek into the past as well as a look into this country's future.

Previous page and these pages: from Hopi Point, at an elevation of some 7,065 feet, can be gained some of the finest views of the intricate windings and craggy cliffs of the Grand Canyon. Overleaf: (left) the green Colorado and red cliffs, near the Unkar Rapids, and (right) bushes cling to the sides of the Grand Canyon.

Previous pages: the Grand Canyon (left) at sunset and (right) from Mather Point on the East Rim Drive. Above: the Grand Canyon from Mohave Point, on the West Rim Drive, and (right) from Yaki Point, overlooking the route taken by the mule trains across the canyon. Overleaf: the scrub-covered upper slopes (left) and the view from Prima Point (right).

Facing page: from Moran Point a clear view can be gained of the rock strata which make up the walls and floors of the Grand Canyon, and of the river tumbling down between the Unkar and the Hance Rapids. Above: the view from Yaki Point. Overleaf: (left) Duck Rock and the Inner Gorge as seen from the West Rim Drive and (right) a splendid sunrise seen from Hopi Point.

Begun in the autumn of 1971, the construction of the village of Tlaquepaque (these pages) was the realization of the dream of Abe Miller, a Nevada businessman who was inspired to build an arts and crafts village in Sedona, Arizona. The fine complex of shops, galleries and restaurants has been largely built in the Spanish Colonial style, which is prevalent among the older buildings of the region.

Above, facing page and overleaf, right: Oak Creek Canyon, one of the finest natural sights to be found on the US 89a, south of Flagstaff. Its dramatically colored cliffs of red and white, steep gorges and strange rock formations make it particularly popular. Overleaf, left: the San Francisco Peaks, further north, which reach 12,670 feet, the highest point in Arizona.

Arizona's Petrified Forest National Park (these pages) takes its name from the many 160-million-year-old logs (facing page) which lie scattered around the park, but the boundaries also take in parts of the Painted Desert (above), where colored rock strata are revealed. Overleaf: (left) Montezuma Castle, one of the many ancient Indian structures in the state, and (right) Navajo Bridge across Marble Canyon.

Above: the precipitous cliffs which tower above the Colorado River at Lee's Ferry, near Page. Further east, straddling the border with Utah, lies the Monument Valley Navajo Tribal Park (facing page and overleaf). The large desert region is best known for its massive sandstone monoliths which rise dramatically into the air and have featured in many a Western movie.

The scenic glories of Monument Valley (these pages and overleaf) belong to the Navajo (overleaf, left), in whose reservation they lie. Closely related to the more warlike Apache, the Navajo are the acknowledged craftsmen of the Southwest, being adept at silverworking, pottery, sand painting and weaving.

Previous pages, left: the Mitten Buttes in Monument Valley. Previous pages right, facing page and overleaf: the spectacular cliffs and isolated monoliths of Canyon de Chelly, in the far northeast of Arizona. This isolated valley has been cultivated by successive tribes of Indians since about AD 350, and is still the home of the Navajo. Above: the Little Colorado River Gorge.

The giant Saguaro cactus (above) can grow to over 40 feet and weigh up to ten tons, yet in their first ten years of life they rarely grow to more than an inch in height. The great size of the cactus is made possible by the far reaching root system which collects every possible drop of moisture available in the desert heat. Facing page: Theodore Roosevelt Lake, east of Phoenix.

Above: the delicate white blooms of the giant Saguaro, which first appear only when the plant is about 50 years old. Other colorful blooms of the Arizona desertlands include: the brilliant red of the Hedgehog Cactus (facing page), the yellow Grizzly Bear Prickly Pear (overleaf, left) and the vividly pink Beaver Tail Cactus (overleaf, right).

These pages: the international resort complex to be found at Lake Havasu City includes London Bridge (above), brought stone by stone from the River Thames and rebuilt across the Colorado, and a typical English pub and phone box (facing page). Overleaf: (left) Saguaro National Monument and (right) Tonto National Monument, which preserves the 700-year-old dwellings of the Salado Indians.

Brooding in the distance, the Superstition Mountains (above) take their name from the legends in which they feature. Facing page: fields of alfalfa are watered by the essential Arizona irrigation system. Overleaf: the Hoover Dam, which impounds one of the largest artificial lakes on the continent and is one of the world's highest dams, reaching 726 feet in height.

Above: the tufa and granite state capitol which stands in the city of Phoenix (facing page), the largest city in Arizona. The city dates back to 1864 when a hay camp was established here, and it has never stopped growing as agricultural and industrial activities continue to expand.

JOHN HEATH
TAKEN FROM
County Jail &
LYNCHED
By Bisbee Mob
IN TOMBSTONE
Feb 22 1884

Facing page: outside Phoenix's St. Mary's Church Jerome Kirk's sculpture of *Phoenix Bird Ascending* rises from a sparkling pool. Above: a grave marker on Boot Hill, in Tombstone (overleaf) the site of the legendary gun battle between the Earps and the Clanton gang in the O.K. Corral.

73

Spanish Missionary activity began around Tucson (these pages and overleaf) in 1692, though the first settlement in Tucson itself only dates back to 1776. Overleaf: (left) the Pima County Court House and (right) Mission San Xavier del Bac, which lies nine miles outside Tucson, has been termed the "White Dove of the Desert" and still ministers to the Papagos Indians as it has since it was built in 1782.

In 1940 Columbia Pictures constructed a frontier town for their film *Arizona* just west of Tucson. Today, it is known as Old Tucson and has become one of the area's main tourist attractions (these pages), featuring recreated fights and stagecoach rides. Overleaf: (left) giant Saguaro in Saguaro National Monument and (right) the mountains of Organ Pipes Cactus National Monument.

Above: Fort Union National Monument. The fort protected the Santa Fe Trail between 1851 and 1891. Facing page: the adobe church at Taos. Overleaf: (left) the Mission of San Miguel, solidly constructed with walls five feet thick, is the oldest church in the U.S.A. (Right) Pueblo de Taos is the tallest Indian pueblo in the Southwest and still houses some 1,400 Indians in traditional homes.

Above: a painting depicting the history of the region from the Conquistadores to the 19th century. Facing page: the high altar of El Santuario de Chimayo, a church built between 1813 and 1816 by local, native craftsmen. Overleaf: (left) traditional dancers at the Pueblo Indian Cultural Center and (right) the church of San Felipe de Neri, built in 1706, in Alberquerque.

Sometime before the birth of Christ, agricultural crops were introduced into the Southwest from Mexico. Over the next 1,300 years the farming culture characterized by irrigation and pueblos flourished, producing Gila Cliff Dwellings (facing page) and the two villages atop El Morro (above). After the 12th century, a prolonged drought, raiding by Apache and Navajo and European diseases destroyed the culture.

Silhouetted by the late evening sun, a lone tree (above) stands in New Mexico's Gila National Forest. Facing page: the sun breaks through the clouds above the Sangre de Cristo Mountains, New Mexico.

Above: Shiprock, which rises 1,700 sheer feet from the desert floor in San Juan County. Facing page: the marvelous interior of the Carlsbad Caverns, deep beneath New Mexico's Guadalupe Mountains. Overleaf: (left) the rugged Hunter Peak in Texas' Guadalupe Mountains National Park and (right) the undulating dunes of the Monahans Sandhills.

On the edge of the Chisos Basin stands the rocky, cloud-shrouded Pulliam Ridge (facing page). Above: the Christmas Mountains of Big Bend National Park, nestled in the arid, rugged and forbidding great curve of the Rio Grande, in southwestern Texas.

The waters of the Rio Grande form the border between Texas and Mexico for hundreds of miles. Along its course the river flows through the fantastic Santa Elena Canyon (facing page), before emptying into Lake Amistad (above). Overleaf: the fine modern architecture of El Paso's Civic Center.

Amarillo (these pages) is most famous as cattle country and the Western Stockyard Auction is held every week as a center for the local ranchers. Overleaf: (left) the Alamo, scene of the heroic stand of Texans in 1836, and (right) the nearby Mission of San Jose, founded in 1720.

Above: the concrete mass of San Antonio's Civic Center, in the northwest quandrant of the HemisFair Plaza. Facing page: a fine view of central San Antonio from atop the Tower of the Americas, a 622-foot-tall concrete spire representing man's desire for new achievement. Overleaf: (left) the Arneson River Theater which, like the bridge (right), is on San Antonio's tree-shaded River Walk.

Facing page: the beautiful pink granite state capitol in Austin, which is the largest in the nation. Above: the gleaming towers of Dallas, from Municipal Plaza Park. Overleaf: Dallas; (righthand page); (right) the Reunion Tower, (left) Thanks-Giving Square, (left hand page); (bottom left) the Hyatt Regency Hotel, (top center) Municipal Plaza Park and (bottom center) the Mobil Building of 1921.

Dallas' Reunion Tower (left) houses a revolving restaurant and cocktail bar which give magnificent views across the "Big D". Behind the tower stands the modern Hyatt Regency Hotel. Facing page: the Central Library at dusk. Overleaf: various views and landmarks in and around Dallas.

Trailways
LOWEST FARE
ANYWHERE
GUARANTEED.

Above: the New City Hall and Reunion Tower at night. Facing page: the center of Dallas from Municipal Plaza Park. Overleaf: (left) dusk-time reflections mirrored in the glass walls of the Lincoln Hotel, one of the newest hotels in Dallas (right).

Fort Worth (these pages) has grown rapidly in recent decades and is now merging with the outskirts of Dallas to form one single megapolis in which the cowpunching tradition can still be felt.

INDEX